A LOOK AT U.S. ELECTIONS

LANDMARK VOTING LAWS

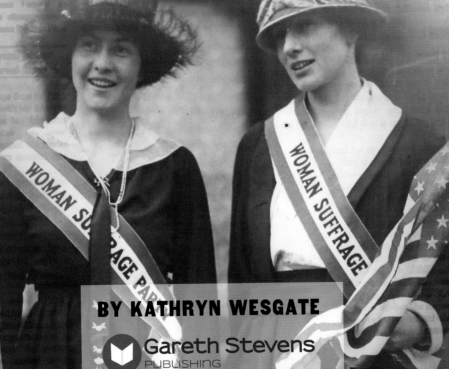

BY KATHRYN WESGATE

Gareth Stevens
PUBLISHING

CRASHCOURSE

Please visit our website, www.garethstevens.com. For a free color catalog of all our high-quality books, call toll free 1-800-542-2595 or fax 1-877-542-2596.

Library of Congress Cataloging-in-Publication Data

Names: Wesgate, Kathryn, author.
Title: Landmark voting laws / Kathryn Wesgate.
Description: New York : Gareth Stevens Publishing, 2021. | Series: A look at U.S. elections | Includes index.
Identifiers: LCCN 2019051299 | ISBN 9781538259641 (library binding) | ISBN 9781538259627 (paperback) | ISBN 9781538259634 (6 Pack) | ISBN 9781538259658 (ebook)
Subjects: LCSH: Election law--United States--Juvenile literature.
Classification: LCC KF4886 . W47 2020 | DDC 342.73/07--dc23
LC record available at https://lccn.loc.gov/2019051299

First Edition

Published in 2021 by
Gareth Stevens Publishing
111 East 14th Street, Suite 349
New York, NY 10003

Editor: Kate Mikoley

Photo credits: Cover, p. 1 Hulton Archive/Getty Images; series art kzww/Shutterstock.com; series art (newspaper) MaryValery/Shutterstock.com; p. 5 Portland Press Herald/Getty Images; p. 7 Hero Images/Getty Images; p. 9 Keith Lance/DigitalVision Vectors/Getty Images; p. 11 Everett Historical/Shutterstock.com; pp. 13, 21 Bettmann/Getty Images; p. 15 Lyndon Baines Johnson Library and Museum/Wikimedia; p. 17 PhotoQuest/Archive Photos/Getty Images; p. 19 Don Carl STEFFEN/Gamma-Rapho/Getty Images; p. 23 Hill Street Studios/DigitalVision/Getty Images; p. 25 fstop123/E+/Getty Images; p. 27 Gilles BASSIGNAC/ Gamma-Rapho/Getty Images; p. 29 Rob Crandall/Shutterstock.com.

Printed in the United States of America

Some of the images in this book illustrate individuals who are models. The depictions do not imply actual situations or events.

CPSIA compliance information: Batch #CS20GS: For further information contact Gareth Stevens, New York, New York at 1-800-542-2595.

Find us on

CONTENTS

Laying Out the Law   4

Amending the Constitution   6

The Nineteenth Amendment   10

The Voting Rights Act of 1965   14

Old Enough to Vote   16

Allowing All to Vote   22

Help America Vote   26

Access to the Polls   28

Timeline of Voting Laws   30

Glossary   31

For More Information   32

Index   32

Words in the glossary appear in **bold** type the first time they are used in the text.

THE LAW

When the **U.S. Constitution** was signed in 1787, it gave states control over how to run elections. At the time, it was almost always white men who owned **property** who could vote. This meant most of the people in the country didn't have their voices heard.

MAKE THE GRADE

An election is the act of voting someone into a government position, such as president or governor.

AMENDING THE CONSTITUTION

New laws and **amendments** to the Constitution have changed how elections work. Today, most **citizens** over 18 can vote, but in the 1860s, most Americans still couldn't vote. Women, African Americans, Native Americans, and Asian Americans were among those not allowed to vote.

MAKE THE GRADE

While the Constitution left elections up to the states, it also gave Congress the power to change these rules as they saw fit.

In 1868, the Fourteenth Amendment gave citizenship to African Americans, but they were still turned away if they tried to vote. In 1870, the Fifteenth Amendment said men couldn't be turned away to vote because of their race or skin color. Still, they were.

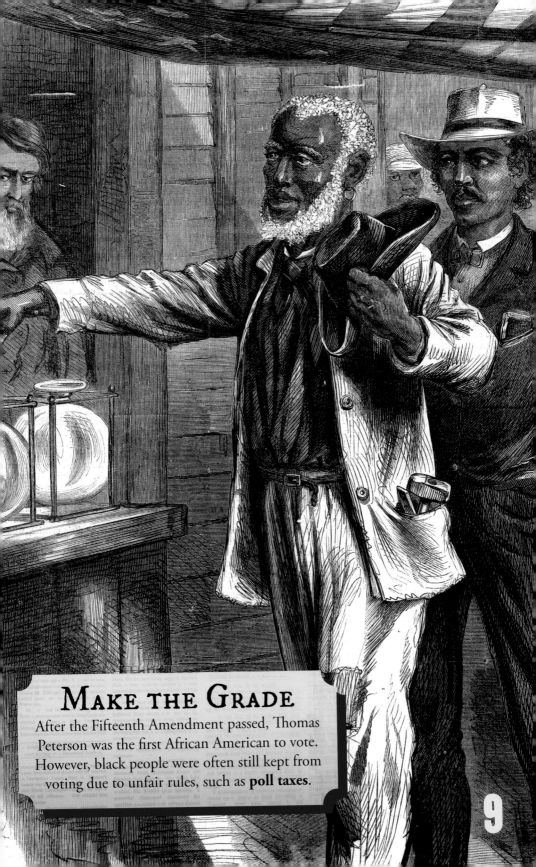

MAKE THE GRADE

After the Fifteenth Amendment passed, Thomas Peterson was the first African American to vote. However, black people were often still kept from voting due to unfair rules, such as **poll taxes**.

THE NINETEENTH AMENDMENT

For nearly 100 years, women in the United States fought for suffrage, or the right to vote. On August 18, 1920, the Nineteenth Amendment was **ratified**. It finally gave women one of the rights white men had for years—the right to vote.

It may seem like the Nineteenth Amendment gave all adult citizens the right to vote. However, unfair rules meant many men and women who weren't white still couldn't vote. For example, in some states you couldn't vote unless your grandfather had voted.

MAKE THE GRADE

Slaves couldn't vote, so the "grandfather clause" meant anyone whose grandparents had been slaves couldn't vote either. At the time, this ruled out many black Americans.

THE VOTING RIGHTS ACT OF 1965

By the 1960s, black men and women were still being kept from voting in the South. In 1964, the Twenty-Fourth Amendment made poll taxes illegal. In 1965, the Voting Rights Act outlawed other methods that kept black people from voting.

MAKE THE GRADE

Civil rights leaders Martin Luther King Jr. and Rosa Parks were among those in the room when President Lyndon B. Johnson signed the Voting Rights Act into law on August 6, 1965.

LYNDON B. JOHNSON

MARTIN LUTHER KING JR.

OLD ENOUGH TO VOTE

During World War II (1939-1945), people had a problem with the voting age. At 18, men could be sent to war, but they still couldn't vote until 21. Young people felt they didn't have any say in the government that was sending them to fight.

Make the Grade

In 1943, Georgia was the first state to lower its voting age to 18 for state and local elections. In **federal** elections, voters still had to be 21.

By the 1960s, the federal voting age still hadn't changed. Now, the United States was fighting the Vietnam War. In 1970, Congress made a change to the Voting Rights Act of 1965. It lowered the voting age to 18 for all federal, state, and local elections.

MAKE THE GRADE

Some people, including President Richard Nixon, thought the change to the Voting Rights Act went against the Constitution. Instead, they thought a Constitutional amendment was needed.

19

In 1971, the Twenty-Sixth Amendment passed. It gave citizens from ages 18 to 20 the right to vote. The amendment was ratified in only 100 days. It was faster than any other amendment had ever been approved.

MAKE THE GRADE

It often takes a while for states to ratify amendments, but five states ratified the Twenty-Sixth Amendment on the same day Congress approved it!

ALLOWING ALL TO VOTE

For a long time, it was hard for people with **disabilities** to vote. Polling places, or buildings where people go to vote, weren't always **accessible**. This made it hard for people who had trouble walking or climbing stairs to get inside to vote. Voting also wasn't accessible for those who had trouble seeing.

22

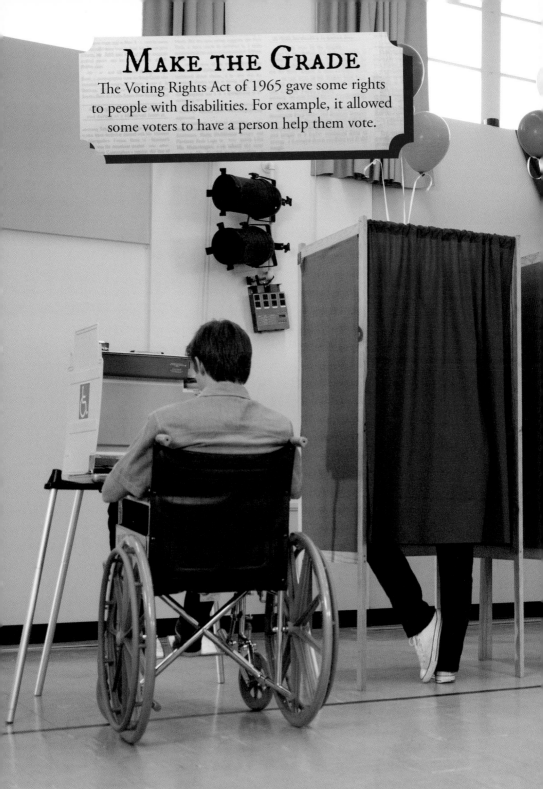

MAKE THE GRADE

The Voting Rights Act of 1965 gave some rights to people with disabilities. For example, it allowed some voters to have a person help them vote.

In 1984, the Voting Accessibility for the Elderly and Handicapped Act required polling places where federal elections were held to be accessible to older voters and those with disabilities. Otherwise, these voters must be given another way to vote.

Voting Today

Voting A-

Make the Grade

The Americans with Disabilities Act of 1990 further required governments make sure people with disabilities had an equal chance to vote.

25

HELP AMERICA VOTE

In 2002, the Help America Vote Act gave voters with disabilities more rights, such as more privacy when voting. The act also gave states more money to be used for elections and created the Election Assistance Commission (EAC), which helps people vote.

MAKE THE GRADE

The Uniformed and Overseas Citizens Absentee Voting Act was passed in 1986 to make it easier for people living overseas or serving in the armed forces to vote.

ACCESS TO THE POLLS

The National Voter Registration Act of 1993 made it easier for voters to register, or sign up, by requiring that states offer multiple ways to do so. While laws have made elections much fairer than they used to be, some still make it hard for people to vote.

Make the Grade

Some people think laws making voters show **identification**, or ID, are unfair because not everyone can easily get ID. Others say it's needed to make sure voters are who they say they are.

TIMELINE OF VOTING LAWS

1787
Constitution gives states control of elections. Only some white men can vote.

1870
Fifteenth Amendment says people cannot be kept from voting because of their race skin color, but many still ar

1920
Nineteenth Amendment gives women the right to vote.

1964
Twenty-Fourth Amendment outlaws poll taxes.

1965
Voting Rights Act bans practices that keep black Americans from voting.

1971
Twenty-Sixth Amendment changes the voting age from 21 to 18.

1984
Voting Accessibility for the Elderly and Handicapped Act is passed.

1993
National Voter Registration Act is passed to make registering to vote easier.

2002
Help America Vote Act is passed.

GLOSSARY

accessible: able to be used by people with disabilities

amendment: a change or addition to a constitution

citizen: someone who lives in a country legally and has certain rights

civil rights: the personal freedoms granted to U.S. citizens by law

disability: a condition that makes it difficult for a person to do certain things

federal: having to do with the national government

identification: a document that shows who a person is and has their name and other information on it

poll tax: a tax people had to pay in order to vote in an election

property: something a person owns, such as land

ratify: to give formal approval of something

slave: a person owned by another person and forced to work without pay

territory: a piece of land that is part of the United States but is not a state

U.S. Constitution: the piece of writing that states the laws of the United States

FOR MORE INFORMATION

BOOKS

Burgan, Michael. *The Voting Rights Act of 1965: An Interactive History Adventure*. North Mankato, MN: Capstone Press, 2015.

Krasner, Barbara. *A Timeline of Presidential Elections*. North Mankato, MN: Capstone Press, 2016

WEBSITES

How Voting Works

www.ducksters.com/history/us_government_voting.php

Find out more about how voting works on this website.

Voting Rights Act of 1965

www.history.com/topics/black-history/voting-rights-act

Learn more about the Voting Rights Act of 1965 here.

Publisher's note to educators and parents: Our editors have carefully reviewed these websites to ensure that they are suitable for students. Many websites change frequently, however, and we cannot guarantee that a site's future contents will continue to meet our high standards of quality and educational value. Be advised that students should be closely supervised whenever they access the internet.

INDEX

amendment 6, 8, 9, 10, 12, 14, 19, 20, 21, 30

Americans with Disabilities Act 25

Congress 7, 18, 21

Constitution 4, 6, 7, 19, 30

Help America Vote Act 26, 30

Johnson, Lyndon B. 15

King, Martin Luther Jr. 15

National Voter Registration Act 28, 30

Nixon, Richard 19

poll taxes 9, 14, 30

polling place 22, 24

suffrage 10

Uniformed and Overseas Absentee Voting Act 27

Voting Accessibility for the Elderly and Handicapped Act 24, 30

voting age 16, 17, 18, 20, 30

Voting Rights Act 14, 15, 18, 19, 23, 30